Why Israel?

Understanding God's Plan
for Israel & the Nations

EZRA FOUNDATION
STUDY · PRACTICE · TEACH

Thomas Fretwell

Why Israel?

Understanding God's Plan for Israel & the Nations

Cover design and layout by: Sarah Fretwell

Printed by: Bishops Printers Ltd, Portsmouth

ISBN: 9781916876804

Published by: Ezra Foundation Press, UK

Please visit our website for more details
www.ezrafoundation.org

Acknowledgements

There are a number of people who have helped me considerably in the completion of this project to whom I would like to express my thanks. Firstly, Jeff Cuozzo for getting behind the vision of the project and supporting it in multiple ways throughout the process. To Philip Bell who did the initial editing on the first manuscript. To all those who kindly read the draft manuscript, provided thoughtful suggestions, and wrote endorsements: Dr. Mitch Glaser, Dr. Daniel Nessim, and Rev. Alex Jacob. Also, to those who proofread the manuscript in its final stages: Charlotte Beveridge and Andrew Fretwell. Finally, to my wife and ministry partner Sarah, for doing a fantastic job on the design of this book.

Endorsements

I am delighted to commend this booklet to you written by Thomas Fretwell. It introduces the reader to a sound biblical theology of the role God has given in scripture to the Jewish people and the land of Israel. It is comprehensive, understandable, biblical and sensitive to the concerns Jewish people oftentimes have about Christianity. As the leader of a global mission to the Jewish people, Chosen People Ministries I highly recommend this booklet to be used and studied as it will inspire and educate those who believe the Bible literally and love the Jewish Messiah Jesus.

Dr Mitch Glaser,
President, Chosen People Ministries (New York)

Why Israel? brings an engaging and informative clarification of the relationship between Israel and the Church. Spanning the breadth of the biblical narrative, Fretwell demonstrates how God has positioned Israel as the key and vehicle of His blessing for all nations.

Dr Daniel Nessim,
Author of *Torah for Gentiles? What the Jewish Authors of the Didache Had to Say*

Thomas Fretwell has served the Church and the wider theological world well in providing excellent teaching and study material. He writes with a well-trained 'theologians eye' complemented by spiritual passion and insight. In Why Israel? he concisely sets out five core truths based largely on a careful exposition of Romans 11:25-29. He also surveys helpfully the 'parting of the ways' and provides helpful historical and theological context to this teaching. I warmly commend these booklets for both private reading and for group study. I trust that many will be challenged, encouraged and equipped by engaging with these resources.

Rev Alex Jacob M.A., M.Phil,
CEO The Churches Ministry Among Jewish People (CMJ UK)

I loved reading this book because it explains vitally important truths regarding God's promises and plans for the nation of Israel in an easy to read and straightforward way. This is a much-needed work, especially for this next generation, who have missed out on much of this sound biblical teaching. As a pastor and ministry leader, I am so thankful to have a concise and uncomplicated resource like this to share with people who have questions about Israel.

Pastor Jeff Cuozzo,
UK & European Coordinator Behold Israel

Contents

I say then, *God* has not rejected His people, has He?
May it never be!

Romans 11:1

Introduction

The Beautiful Land

King David famously cried out in prayer, "And what one nation on earth is like Your people Israel" (1 Chronicles 17:20). Moses wrote that Israel is "a land for which the Lord your God cares; the eyes of the Lord are always on it" (Deuteronomy 11:12). God, through the prophet Ezekiel, described the land of Israel as the "glory of all lands" (Ezekiel 20:6). Such statements, found so frequently throughout the Bible, may be puzzling to some people. What do statements such as these actually mean? Are the people of Israel better than other peoples? Is the Land of Israel really comparable to the majestic sight of the Canadian Rockies, the golden sands of the Caribbean, or the beauty of the Great Barrier Reef? Its size cannot compare to the vast plains of the Serengeti or the splendour of the Grand Canyon. It is a small stretch of land that boasts very few natural resources compared to those surrounding it. For many it is a land that is synonymous with war, conflict and strife. So, what are we as Christians to make of such statements?

In spite of its troubles, the Land of Israel has a magnetic quality, a mysterious aura that is as compelling as it is elusive.

It is a land revered by people all over the globe, steeped in history, and which people are willing to fight and die for. It is also a land where East meets West, sitting at the crossroads of the continents. Furthermore, it is a land full of lush vegetation but also barren wilderness, both beauty and desolation. It is truly a unique land in many ways.

But ultimately the land and people of Israel are unique for a deeper and much more significant reason. There is a supernatural element that must be included to properly understand what makes Israel so unique, and it is this that lies behind the elusive attraction so often associated with this land. The Jewish people are unique in that they were birthed out of a covenant. God made this covenant with Abraham thousands of years ago. It is an everlasting covenant that forever binds the Jewish people and the land of Israel to God. It is why God often uses the expression "My people Israel" (Ezekiel 36:8) in the Bible, and He can talk of Israel as "My land":

> I brought you into the fruitful land, to eat its
> fruit and its good things. But you came and
> defiled My land, and my inheritance you
> made an abomination.
> **Jeremiah 2:7**

> The land, moreover, shall not be sold
> permanently, for the land is mine
> **Leviticus 25:23**

The land of Israel is forever entwined with the people of Israel and the two cannot be separated. For, as Baruch Maoz explains:

> "Israel denotes both people and the land... the Land is no passive observer, a mere sphere in which Israel as a people operate. It is spoken of as altogether at one with the people."[1]

This explains why, throughout Jewish history, especially during periods of exile, there has been a consistent longing for the land of Israel. During the days of the Babylonian captivity the psalmist of Israel wrote, "How shall we sing the Lord's song in a foreign land? If I forget you, O Jerusalem, let my right hand forget its skill" (Psalm 137:4-5). Ever since the Temple was destroyed and the Jews entered the period known as the diaspora (dispersed from the land), still the longing to return has remained in their hearts. For nearly two thousand years the Jewish Passover ceremony has concluded with the words "Next year in Jerusalem". This longing has been beautifully expressed by Jewish author Ernst Frankenstein during one of the most devastating periods of Israel's history – the dark night of the Holocaust:

> "For the Jews, Palestine is not just a land. It is the only land on earth which really matters. Given to them by divine promise, returned to them after the Babylonian captivity, liberated under the great Maccabean leaders, mourned for eighteen centuries, goal of all their dreams and hopes, of prayers and songs, it cannot be separated from the life of the Jewish people. The people may exist in other countries, as it had to exist through the long centuries of dispersion. But it will only live in Palestine."[2]

The subject of Israel is intricately woven into the theological fabric of the biblical narrative and is perhaps the largest subject contained within the Bible. The Land of Israel is that of the patriarchs and the prophets: the land promised to Abraham, Isaac and Jacob; the land where Elijah and Elisha, Jeremiah and Isaiah prophesied to the children of Israel. It is a land of miracles, where the River Jordan parted, and the walls of Jericho came crashing down. It is the land of the psalmists: it was here that David, Asaph and the sons of Korah composed the sweet songs of Israel. It is the land of the famed kings of Israel and Judah, such as David, Solomon, and Hezekiah.

Here they reigned over the nation and constructed the great
Jewish Temples. Ultimately, it is the land where God dwelt;
His Glory cloud, His presence, resting upon the mercy seat of
the Ark of the Covenant that occupied the Holy of Holies in
the Temple edifice.

For Christians too, the land holds special significance. This is
the land where the "Word became flesh and dwelt among us"
(John 1:14). It is the land of Jesus, the Messiah. It was here, in
Bethlehem, that the Messiah was born. In Nazareth he grew
up, and on the shores of the Sea of Galilee He conducted his
public ministry. His teaching was saturated with imagery
drawn from the land and its people. On its streets He
performed miracles: making the blind see, the lame walk, the
deaf hear, and raising the dead to life (Luke 7:22). It was the
soil of Gethsemane that soaked up His tears and the ground of
Golgotha that absorbed His blood. Finally, it was in this land
that the Son of God was crucified for the sins of the world.
It was here, from the Mount of Olives in Jerusalem that He
ascended into heaven to sit at the right hand of the Father. It is
also to this very place that one day He is destined to return –
the Bible records that His feet will touch the Mount of Olives
and it will be split in two (Zechariah 14:4). Truly this makes
the Land of Israel unique. There is no other land on earth that
can claim things such as this. It is truly the Lord's land.

The Eternal Jew

Years ago, the novelist Leo Tolstoy asked this question:

"What is the Jew?"

He answered:

"The Jew is the symbol of eternity. ... He is the one who for so long had guarded the prophetic message and transmitted it to all mankind. A people such as this can never disappear. The Jew is eternal. He is the embodiment of eternity."[3]

It is not just the land that is unique – it is the people too. History can give us nothing that is even remotely comparable to the history of the Jews. It is one of wonder and tragedy, defying all worldly explanations. Stretching back some 4000 years to the Patriarch Abraham, it is traced forwards in time through his son Isaac, his grandson Jacob, then Jacob's twelve sons, the years of slavery in Egypt, the wilderness wanderings under Moses, the taking of the Promised Land under Joshua, the rise of the monarchy under Saul and David, the splitting of the kingdom into North (Israel) and South (Judah), the Assyrian and Babylonian captivities, and the long waited return to the land under Ezra and Nehemiah.

This unbroken story of the Jewish people continued into the days of the Maccabees and their heroic fight for freedom. Then came the mighty Roman Empire, yet still the Jews remained. During Roman occupation the birth, death and resurrection of Jesus took place. The story continues with the great Jewish war of AD 70, when the temple was destroyed and the Jewish people were scattered throughout the world. Yet, unlike most nations of history who have been conquered and exiled among the nations, the Jewish people maintained their distinct identity. Their story continues through the worldwide diaspora, the times of the great sages of Israel and into the Talmudic era [4].

And now we continue to witness the story in our day: the re-establishment of the State of Israel (1948) after nearly 1900 years and the regathering of Jews from the diaspora is nothing short of miraculous. There is no precedent in history for something like this. In fact, there really is no earthly explanation – except the fact that God made a covenant with Abraham all those millennia ago.

This unique history has not gone unnoticed, the famous quote by Mark Twain puts it best:

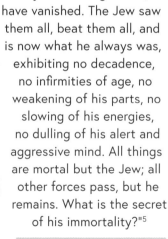

"The Egyptian, the Babylonian, and the Persian rose, filled the planet with sound and splendour, then faded to dream-stuff and passed away; the Greek and the Roman followed; and made a vast noise, and they are gone; other people have sprung up and held their torch high for a time, but it burned out, and they sit in twilight now, or have vanished. The Jew saw them all, beat them all, and is now what he always was, exhibiting no decadence, no infirmities of age, no weakening of his parts, no slowing of his energies, no dulling of his alert and aggressive mind. All things are mortal but the Jew; all other forces pass, but he remains. What is the secret of his immortality?"[5]

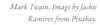

Mark Twain, Image by Jackie Ramirez from Pixabay.

Well, quite simply the secret of their 'immortality', their longevity as a distinct people, is the God of Israel. They are a covenant people and their history cannot be understood apart from God. When the Lord appeared to Abraham, he said to him:

"I am God Almighty; Walk before Me, and be blameless. I will establish My covenant between Me and you, and I will multiply you exceedingly." Abram fell on his face, and God talked with him, saying, "As for Me, behold, My covenant is with you, and you will be the father of a multitude of nations. No longer shall your name be called Abram, but your name shall be Abraham; For I have made you the father of a multitude of nations. I will make you exceedingly fruitful, and I will make nations of you, and kings will come forth from you. I will establish My covenant between Me and you and your descendants after you throughout their generations for an everlasting covenant, to be God to you and to your descendants after you."
Genesis 17:1-7

The history of Israel is unrivalled in world affairs. It is a history that has seen some of the darkest nights of the human soul, witnessed the brutality of persecution throughout the globe, yet at the same time has fulfilled the promise of Abraham to bless all the nations. For out of this nation came One who changed the world. Although often unseen by Jews today, the story of Israel is a story of their Messiah – Jesus. In many ways it is a history that was written down beforehand. There are no other nations whose history and destiny were mapped out and prophesied in such a detailed manner in the Bible. This is another reason why Israel is unique: what we regard as history was divinely foretold for all to read, often centuries beforehand; and importantly, much of this prophetic history remains to be fulfilled.

Often when the subject of Israel is discussed it is accompanied by a barrage of pointed questions, uniformed opinions, diverse theological arguments and heated emotions. People want to hold an informed view but are often unsure where to start. The baggage of modern geo-political concerns clouds people's thinking about Israel.

It is important to make sure that we have the proper theological foundation before we start interpreting current events. The problem is most people have no biblical theology of Israel by which they can correctly assess the claims they are hearing. Among the younger generations particularly there is ambiguity about the place of Israel in the plan of God. Bestselling author Joel Rosenberg, commentating on a recent LifeWay survey measuring evangelical attitudes toward Israel, made the following remark about the millennial generation:

"The survey makes it clear that many of them really don't understand Israel's place in the biblical narrative."[6]

This is a problem that the Ezra Foundation (a non-denominational Christian organisation) seeks to address, by providing a new generation of believers with biblically faithful answers to their questions about Israel. In order to achieve this, the entire subject of Israel needs to be seen for what it is in the Bible—perhaps the largest metanarrative in all of Scripture. The topic of Israel needs to be treated as a biblical theology theme that runs throughout the entire Bible, for it addresses the past, present and future role of the Jewish people in the plan of God. In setting out a biblical theology of Israel, which will incorporate periods of exile, periods of unbelief, and even anticipate an eschatological kingdom, we seek to offer a theology that affirms the unique role of Israel in salvation history. At the same time, we want to avoid the error of placing the modern State of Israel beyond all criticism. To hold a view that acknowledges God's heart for the Jewish people does *not* mean one is bound to support every decision of the secular Israeli Government today.

This booklet aims to outline a biblical theology of Israel as found in chapter eleven of Paul's epistle to the Romans. During this brief exposition, other topics of interest will be interspersed throughout. This should give readers a basic overview of the issues that emerge as you study this topic in the Bible.

A Biblical Theology of Israel from Romans 11:25-29

For I do not want you, brethren, to be uninformed of this mystery—so that you will not be wise in your own estimation—that a partial hardening has happened to Israel until the fullness of the Gentiles has come in; and so all Israel will be saved; just as it is written,
"The Deliverer will come from Zion,
He will remove ungodliness from Jacob."
"This is My covenant with them,
When I take away their sins."
From the standpoint of the gospel they are enemies for your sake, but from the standpoint of God's choice they are beloved for the sake of the fathers; for the gifts and the calling of God are irrevocable.
Romans 11:25-29

Although this section of Romans is the final portion of a much larger section of chapters 9-11, which expounds upon the subject of God's dealings with Israel, it provides us with five truths that provide the backbone of a basic biblical theology of Israel.

Truth One:

Israel is often misunderstood by the *Church*

1

For I do not want you, brethren, to be uninformed
of this mystery—so that you will not be
wise in your own estimation
Romans 11:25a

The text states that the Church must be careful not to display an attitude of ignorance concerning Israel's current position of blindness, nor are we to allow this position to produce in us an attitude of superiority or arrogance. Unfortunately, as far as Israel is concerned, the ugly mixture of ignorance and arrogance is an apt description of the Church's attitude for much of its history, indicating that Paul's warning has gone largely unheeded. The theological position known as Replacement Theology (or Supersessionism) has been the majority view from about the fourth century onwards, only really losing its dominance in the eighteenth century. The idea is essentially that the Church has replaced Israel in the future plan of God. Those who hold this view believe that the covenantal promises regarding Israel's future have now been transferred to the Church—it has become the new "spiritual Israel." This position quickly became the dominant stance of the post-Apostolic Church. And as the influence of supersessionism grew, it brought with it a shameful legacy of Christian antisemitism that persisted, and some would say culminated, in the terrible events of the 20th century.

Confronting Theological Antisemitism

It would not be an accurate characterisation to imply that everyone who holds to some form of replacement theology is guilty of antisemitism, that is definitely not the case. Yet, at the same time, as biblical scholar Michael Vlach concludes, "it is undeniable that anti-Jewish bias has often gone hand in hand with the supersessionist view".[7] As Jewish authors Prager and Telushkin note, "Christianity did not create the Holocaust... but it made it possible. Without Christian antisemitism, the Holocaust would have been inconceivable".[8] They continue that for, "nearly two thousand years...the Christian world dehumanized the Jew, ultimately helping lay the groundwork for the Holocaust".[9] Much of the external imagery that is associated with traditional antisemitic actions tragically owe their origin not to the Third Reich or the Muftis (Islamic jurists), but to the Church. The ghettos, enforced wearing of yellow stars and identification badges, pointy hats, segregation, banishments, job restrictions and synagogue burnings all had a distressing historical precedent throughout Christendom.[10]

A look at a small number of the publications produced throughout church history witnesses to this fact. Hippolytus

(AD 160-235) wrote a volume called *"Expository Treatise against the Jews"* which called the Jewish people a perverse race. The bishop of Constantinople, John Chrysostom (AD 345-405) preached a series of sermons entitled *"Orations against the Jews"* which attacked the Jewish people with such vehemence they stand today as a contender for the most anti-Semitic writings in history. To Chrysostom, the synagogue is a "whorehouse" and "a den of thieves", the Jews are "no better than pigs and goats in their lewd grossness", they are also "lustful, rapacious, greedy, perfidious, bandits ... inveterate murderers, men possessed by the devil". Finally, Chrysostom declared that "God has always hated the Jews, [and] it is incumbent upon all Christians to hate the Jews".[11]

The following centuries were marked by numerous vicious blood libels, the demonising of the Jews and institutionalised antisemitism, a malicious pattern that sadly continued all through the medieval period. The reformation leader Martin Luther, initially seen as favourable towards the Jews, continued the *Adversus Judaeos* tradition with his 1542 tract *"Against the Jews and their Lies"*,

Martin Luther (1483–1546), oil painting.
Gift of Robert Lehman, 1955 (CC-BY-2.5).

25

where he proposed that their synagogues "should be set on fire" for "the honour of God and Christianity".[12]

After the tragic events of the Holocaust many churches actively sought to remove any trace of replacement theology from their midst. For the most part this led to a successful reappraisal of Christian theology in this area. However, Christians need to be aware that a new form of replacement theology has been gaining popularity in the evangelical church in recent times. This runs the risk of reviving the shameful legacy of Christian antisemitism and it must be challenged.

One social commentator suggests that the ancient doctrine of supersessionism, which had only been supressed after the Holocaust, has now "been revived under the influence of the Middle East conflict".[13] This resurgence has been inflamed by the ongoing Israeli-Palestinian conflict and the support of those who advocate imposing a social justice narrative onto the Scriptures. This portrays the Palestinians as helpless underdogs trying to resist the might of their imperialist overlords—Israel! This movement is known as "The New Supersessionism," and it fuses together traditional replacement doctrines with Palestinian nationalism and liberation theology. The movement is unapologetically anti-Zionist in its politics. This is where a new problem has arisen. The line between anti-Zionism and antisemitism has become dangerously blurred. Too often the two are seen as one and the same. Antisemitism sheltering under the banner of anti-

Zionism is now referred to as 'The New Antisemitism'. Israel is now seen as the collective Jew and can be hated all the same. The late Professor Robert Wistrich was the world's foremost authority on antisemitism, as the head of the International Centre for Antisemitism at the Hebrew University. He put it this way:

"You have the denial, for instance, that there is any relationship between so-called criticism of Israel and anti-Semitism, but, in fact, most of what goes by the name of criticism of Israel is feeding on a daily basis the growing demonization of the Jewish state, which in turn spills over, I would say, almost with mathematical inevitability into some form of dislike, hostility, or even loathing of Jews."[14]

Of course, it is critically important to realize that within a democracy, albeit an imperfect democracy, criticism of Israel can be important for positive change. A *valid*, albeit negative, criticism of Israeli policy should not be considered antisemitic. In a government consisting of both religious and secular groups, including those on the left and the right, you will not find fiercer debate about Israeli policies than within Israel itself. But where this criticism involves an attempt to demonize and delegitimize the State of Israel by applying double standards, this may properly be identified as the New Antisemitism. Evangelical theology should be able to stand squarely against any form of antisemitism, whether it is directed at Jews individually or against Israel collectively, whether it surfaces under the guise of politics or theology.

Why the Jewish People?

Professor Robert Wistrich also described antisemitism as "The Longest Hatred" and traced examples of it through from the beginning of Jewish history to the present day. There is ultimately no reasonable "natural" explanation for why this is the case. The answer lies in the spiritual realm. The Apostle Paul writes in the book of Romans about his Jewish kinsmen that to them:

belongs the adoption as sons, and the glory and the covenants and the giving of the Law and the temple service and the promises, whose are the fathers, and from whom is the Christ according to the flesh, who is over all, God blessed forever. Amen
Romans 9:4-5

In this passage, we are told that the covenants belong to the Jewish people. This is a pivotal point to understand. The biblical covenants explain how God mediates His blessings to the world. The Abrahamic Covenant (Genesis 12:1-3; 15:18-21), the Davidic Covenant (2 Samuel 7:8-14) and the New Covenant (Jeremiah 31:31-34) contain God's promises to bless the children of Israel with a Land and a Royal seed, who would go on to bless the entire world with the forgiveness of sins. The covenants contain the promises of God, the promises of God display His character and nature, and the covenants were given to the House of Israel.

Here is the connection that explains why such disproportionate hatred is directed toward the Jews (considering the actual Jewish population size) – They are God's covenant people and continue to be to this day (Romans 11:1). These covenants affirm the continuing place and purpose for Israel in God's redemptive kingdom program, even while being in a state of unbelief (Romans 11:25). The satanic onslaught against the Jewish people is reflective of the attempt by Satan to discredit God by showing that His promises can be broken. Satan being the "prince of the power of the air" (Ephesians 2:2) and the "god of this world" (2 Corinthians 4:4) mobilizes the masses in pursuit of his goal. Such ambitions are expressed by the ancient enemies of Israel in Psalm 83, and similar sentiments could be listed from a number of world leaders today:

> They make shrewd plans against Your people,
> and conspire together against Your treasured
> ones. They have said, "Come, and let us wipe
> them out as a nation, that the name of
> Israel be remembered no more."
> **Psalm 83:3-4**

Satan has tried to wipe out the Jewish people through many different means over the years. The Egyptians, the Amalekites, the Babylonians, the Hittites, the Assyrians, and the Romans. Through individuals like Haman and Hitler. Through the Russian pogroms and the Nazis in the twentieth century. Satan has attempted to use religions and politics in his nefarious quest. Yet we can have full assurance that Satan will never succeed. In Jeremiah 31 God identifies Himself as the Creator of the sun, moon and stars where He states emphatically that, only if someone can remove these ordinances, will they be able to destroy the Jews. In other words, it is impossible – the existence of the Jewish people is a testimony to God's enduring faithfulness to keep His promises:

> "If this fixed order departs from before Me,"
> declares the LORD, "Then the offspring of
> Israel also will cease from being a nation
> before Me forever."
> **Jeremiah 31:36**

Truth Two:

The hardening of *Israel* is
partial and temporary

2

> For I do not want you, brethren, to be uninformed
> ... that a partial hardening has happened to Israel
> until the fullness of the Gentiles has come in
> **Romans 11:25**

Everyone that seeks to grapple with the question of Israel will sooner or later have to confront the reality of Israel's present-day unbelief. It is true, the vast majority of Jews reject the idea that Jesus is the Messiah. Church history shows that Gentile Christendom has often reacted against charges of anti-Jewish bias by pointing out that the Jewish people rejected Christ and are presently unbelievers.

The Apostle Paul in the above verse seems to pre-empt this response by explaining the reason for Israel's present hardness. Paul had previously explained the reason for God allowing Israel to stumble; it was "by their transgression that salvation has come to the Gentiles" (Romans 11:11). In other words, it was for our benefit; therefore Paul warns Christian churches, "do not be arrogant toward the branches" (11:18). Here he reaffirms his interpretation of Israel's current position as the result of divine hardening. He emphasizes that the current hardening is only "partial," for there remains a faithful remnant of believers within the nation; "there has also come to be at the present time a remnant according to *God's* gracious choice" (11:5), Paul himself being one of them. This remnant is evidence of God's continued faithfulness to Israel, which proves the nation has not been rejected.

The Remnant – Messianic Jewish Identity

Although the term Messianic Jew is a relatively new one, throughout history many other names have been used to describe the remnant of believing Jews that the Apostle Paul refers to. Some of these names include Hebrew Christians, Jewish Christians and Nazarenes. Regardless of the particular designation they are all used to refer to someone who is ethnically Jewish and has come to believe that Yeshua (Jesus) is the Jewish Messiah promised in the Law and the prophets. They still self-identify as Jews and seek to incorporate many elements of Jewish practice with their faith in Jesus.

There is a widely held misconception today that if a Jewish person accepts Jesus as their Messiah then they somehow forfeit their Jewish identity. Part of the confusion on this matter comes from the various different ways in which people try to define what it means to be a Jew. Some will use religion to define Jewishness, for some it is hereditary, still others may use nationalism. However, for our purposes we will seek to offer an objective standard for defining Jewishness – the scriptures. The biblical basis for defining Jewishness is derived from lineal descent of the patriarchs Abraham, Isaac and Jacob, as outlined in the Abrahamic covenant (Genesis 12:1-3, Genesis 15:45, Genesis 26:2-5). The Apostle Paul recognised this when he wrote:

> I say then, God has not rejected His people, has He? May it never be! For I too am an Israelite, a descendant of Abraham, of the tribe of Benjamin
> **Romans 11:1**

Paul described himself as a "Hebrew of Hebrews" (Philippians 3:5), and in his defence before the Jews in the book of Acts he says this:

> I am a Jew, born in Tarsus of Cilicia, but brought up in this city, educated under Gamaliel, strictly according to the law of our fathers, being zealous for God just as you all are today
> **Acts 22:3**

He nowhere gives any indication that his acceptance of Jesus as Messiah had any effect on his (Paul's) Jewish identity. The same holds true today. Based on this biblical definition, whether a Jewish person is ultra-orthodox, a follower of Karl Marx, a committed atheist, or a believer in Jesus, nothing they can do will change the fact that they are Jewish; they are descendants of Abraham, Isaac and Jacob, regardless of what various groups may try to say. This ongoing unique Jewish identity is an important witness to the unity between Jew and Gentile in the body of Christ through the Messiah and a testimony to the faithfulness of God to keep his promises.

Unfortunately, early developments in Judaism, and slightly later in Christianity too, have propounded the false view that believing in Jesus somehow means you forfeit Jewish identity. The origins of Christianity are entirely Jewish. The Jesus movement of the first century began as a sect within Judaism. Jesus and his early followers were all Jewish, they spoke Hebrew and Aramaic, they worshiped at the Temple in Jerusalem (until it was destroyed), they taught at synagogues around Israel, observed Jewish holidays, practiced Jewish traditions, and anticipated the coming Davidic Kingdom under the rule of the Jewish King. Their teaching is saturated with Jewish imagery and references to Jewish history.

Jesus himself, during the early days of His public ministry, chose the setting to identify Himself as the Messiah. It was during a shabbat (Sabbath) synagogue service in Nazareth when Jesus was called to approach the bema (pulpit) and read from the haftarah portion (weekly reading) of the prophet Isaiah. The Gospel of Luke records this event as follows:

And the book of the prophet Isaiah was handed to Him. And He opened the book and found the place where it was written, "The Spirit of the Lord is upon Me, because He anointed Me to preach the gospel to the poor. He has sent Me to proclaim release to the captives, and recovery of sight to the blind, to set free those who are oppressed, to proclaim the favorable year of the Lord." And He closed the book, gave it back to the attendant and sat down; and the eyes of all in the synagogue were fixed on Him. And He began to say to them, "Today this Scripture has been fulfilled in your hearing."

Luke 4:17-21

Jesus here claims to be fulfilling the mission of the Messianic figure described in Isaiah. It is a provocative claim, yes to some, but it is also significant that he chose perhaps the most thoroughly Jewish setting one could imagine for this announcement (cf. Luke 4:16).

The issue for the early disciples of Jesus was not what happens to Jews who become believers, but what happens in the case of Gentiles becoming believers. This dilemma actually led to the convening of the first Church council in Jerusalem where it was decided that non-Jews were able to follow Jesus without the need to practice Judaism (Acts 15). The gospel was to go out from Jerusalem to the corners of the earth. It was good news to both Jews and non-Jews. This view gradually became inverted over time as the Church became increasingly Gentile in its makeup.

Jew and Gentile in One Body?

So how did a predominately Jewish Church become largely Gentile? It happened gradually over the course of a few centuries but there are some specific events that contributed to this period of history, known as "the parting of the ways". The major contributing factors were the Jewish revolts of AD 70 and 135. Firstly, in the years leading up to AD 70 as the Roman siege of Jerusalem intensified, and the early Jewish disciples recalled the words of Jesus in Matthew 24:16 to "flee to the mountains", they obediently left the city when the opportunity arose. Such actions were viewed as traitorous by the wider Jewish community.

The second Jewish revolt further separated the two communities. When the second revolt against Rome began, under the leadership of Bar-Kokhba, the influential Rabbi Akiva pronounced him to be the Messiah. This meant that to support this revolt would be to support a false Messiah which the Jewish followers of Jesus could not do, so they withdrew their support. Although the rebellion was quashed by the Romans, the actions of the Jewish believers were not forgotten – the rift between the two communities grew larger.

Then sometime during the second century, as Talmudic Judaism was established, the rabbinic leaders wanted to draw a line between who was and who wasn't part of the Jewish community. Jewish believers in Jesus were not welcome at this point and there was a 'benediction' called the *Birkat HaMinin* (benediction of the apostates) added to the Amidah liturgy that called for the destruction of apostates – of which the Messianic Jews were now considered a guilty party.[15] An early copy of this benediction was found in the Cairo synagogue and it reads:

> "May the Nazarenes ... instantly perish: may they be blotted from the book of the living."[16]

As believers were unwilling to say this part of the liturgy they were easily identified and put out of the synagogue. As Jewish life now centred around the synagogue and not the Temple, this basically meant that Jewish believers could not be part of the larger Jewish community.

One of the indirect consequences of the Bar-Kokhba rebellion was the issuing of a decree from the Roman leader Hadrian (AD 132) which forbade Jews from coming within sight of Jerusalem. This had huge ramifications for the Jerusalem Church and led to a marginalisation of Jewish influence. As

Gentiles became dominant within the Church, they brought with them Greek allegorical methods of biblical interpretation, along with the antisemitism of the Greco-Roman world. This led to the rise of replacement theology and the beginning of a long history of Christian antisemitism.

For instance, the first council of Nicaea, convened by Emperor Constantine (AD 325) to codify the Church's teaching on the nature of Christ, was problematic in many ways for the Jews. The Nicene Creed, which came out of the council, is a strong affirmation of the deity of Christ. However, what is less well known about the council in Christian circles is the harsh anti-Jewish laws that were passed at this time too. These laws made it very difficult to believe in Jesus while maintaining an outward Jewish identity. Jewish people who believed in Jesus were required to stop celebrating the feasts and practicing Jewish customs; rather they were to conform to Greco-Roman culture, even taking new "Christian" names. This is also when the Jewish calendar was abandoned by the Church. Easter was instituted to make sure that Christians did not have to share the festival with the Jewish Passover. The Council stated: "For it is unbecoming beyond measure that on this holiest of festivals we should follow the customs of the Jews. Henceforth let us have nothing in common with this odious people..."[17]

Messianic Jews at this time were both ejected from the wider Jewish community and forced to abandon their Jewishness and assimilate into the Church. Unfortunately, this council set the precedent for many similar anti-Judaic restrictions that would be passed at subsequent councils.

In spite of this, there has always been a remnant of Jewish believers throughout the centuries. Most recently, in the twentieth century the modern Messianic movement has grown considerably. With a rising Christian missionary focus on Jewish evangelism in the nineteenth century, and the reestablishment of the state of Israel in the twentieth, Messianic Jews are once again able to maintain their Jewish identity and express their faith in Jesus in authentically Jewish ways.

The Hardening of Israel is Temporary

Let us return to the text in Romans 11:25. Paul has stated the hardening is only a partial one, explaining the presence of the believing Jewish remnant throughout history. However, the real content of the "mystery" (Romans 11:25) is not just that a remnant in the nation would remain, as this concept is already found in the Old Testament. Neither is the mystery the fact that Israel would one day experience a national revival beyond the locus of a small remnant, as this too is clearly taught in the Old Testament. Rather, what qualifies this aspect of Pauline teaching as a mystery is that "the inauguration of the eschatological age would involve setting aside the majority of Jews while Gentiles streamed in to enjoy the blessings of salvation and that only when that stream had been exhausted would Israel as a whole experience these blessings."[18]

This period within the larger context of salvation history is set to continue *"until the fullness of the Gentiles comes in"*. The word "until" in this context definitively indicates an end of one situation and the commencement of another. The term is reminiscent of the words of Jesus to the people of Israel when He said:

> For I say to you, from now on you will not see Me until you say, "Blessed is He who comes in the name of the Lord!"
> **Matthew 23:39**

Paul is saying that this present position of hardening will exist until the full number of Gentiles have come to believe in Jesus as their Messiah. The "fullness of the Gentiles" is this present age when God is "taking from among the Gentiles a people for His name" (Acts 15:14). The phrase is closely related to Jesus' expression "the times of the Gentiles" in Luke 21:24. The former ("fullness") seems to have a numerical focus whilst the latter is chronologically focused. The termination of the fullness of the Gentiles quantitatively would seem to be the time when Jesus returns (cf. Acts 15:14-16, Luke 21:24-27). Paul's brief sketch of salvation history, then, includes unbelieving Israel in the present age, and this must factor into any biblical theology concerning Israel.

Truth Three:

Israel *will* experience national regeneration

> and so all Israel will be saved; just as it is written,
> "The Deliverer will come from Zion, He will
> remove ungodliness from Jacob."
> "This is My covenant with them,
> when I take away their sins."
> **Romans 11:26-27**

The little phrase "all Israel shall be saved" has caused much debate in the Church. Several possible interpretations have been offered by theologians. Some see "Israel" here as pertaining to the elect, the one people of God comprising both believing Jews and Gentiles. This position seems doubtful given that Paul has used the term consistently ten times throughout Romans 9-11 to refer to ethnic Israel. Others have claimed that "all Israel" is to be understood as a reference to all Jews throughout history. This position, however, raises a variety of soteriological problems and does not fit the context of the discussion. Still, others simply see this as a reference to the elect within Israel who are now part of the Church.

The multitude of interpretations only shows how problematic the Church's theology of Israel has become. Rather than engage with all of these viewpoints, I will argue for the view that seems to be the most straightforward. If we read it without any preconceived assumptions inherited from our particular theological systems, then some of the confusion evaporates. To interpret "all Israel" as a reference to the ethnic nation of Israel seems to fit the context best. To understand the words "will be saved" as a reference to the national salvation of Israel fits easily with the overall narrative of Israel given to us in the scriptures. The national regeneration and eschatological salvation of Israel is one of the most frequently recorded hopes of the prophets (cf. Ezekiel 37:25-28; Jeremiah 31:31-34; Micah 4:1-4). The great British clergymen Bishop J.C. Ryle said it well, and his comments are all the more significant given that he wrote this prior to 1948 when modern Israel was established in their homeland.

"But time would fail me, if I attempted to quote all the passages of Scripture in which the future history of Israel is revealed. Isaiah, Jeremiah, Ezekiel, Hosea, Joel, Amos, Obadiah, Micah, Zephaniah, Zechariah all declare the same thing. All predict, with more or less particularity, that in the end of this dispensation the Jews are to be restored to their own land and to the favour of God. I lay no claim to infallibility in the interpretation of Scripture in this matter. I am well aware that many excellent Christians

> cannot see the subject as I do. I can only say,
> that to my eyes, the future salvation of Israel as a
> people, their return to Palestine and their national
> conversion to God, appear as clearly and plainly
> revealed as any prophecy in God's Word."[19]

Paul seems to emphasize this point by his selection of Old Testament quotations. He first quotes a verse from Isaiah 59:20. The context is crucial; Isaiah 59 is an eschatological chapter dealing with the second coming of Christ in judgment at the end of the age, to repay those whose deeds are wicked. This same chapter describes Jesus as a "redeemer" who will come to Zion (location) and remove the sins of Israel (ethnicity). The next verse (Isaiah 59:21) links these events, the salvation of ethnic Israel to the New Covenant. This is supported by the second Old Testament quote that Paul selects from Jeremiah 31:33-34 where he explicitly ties the salvation of Israel to the New Covenant.

Most theologians today would not deny that the New Covenant awaits its final consummation with the coming of Christ. The New Covenant is not something that appears only in the New Testament – it was predicted in the Hebrew scriptures first, and then instituted by Jesus with his famous words at the Passover meal he celebrated with his disciples; "This cup which is poured out for you is the new covenant in My blood" (Luke 22:20). Every time we take communion, we are remembering this covenant. Such familiarity with it has often led to a triumphalist approach on behalf of the Church because there is a tendency for Christians to think it is a covenant that was made solely with the Church; that is, a new thing, now that the old Mosaic covenant has expired. We need to be very careful here, since the Bible teaches that even the New Covenant was made with the House of Israel and not the Church.

Now it is true that, through the grace of God, the Gentiles have been blessed to share in the spiritual blessings of the New Covenant and experience the benefits of salvation and the indwelling Holy Spirit which are available to all people today through the gospel and this is what we celebrate through communion. But Paul here is highlighting that there is more to the New Covenant than individual salvation; the fullness of the New Covenant includes the national regeneration of Israel. Not only this, but the New Covenant also includes the fulfilment of the Land promises originally given to Israel in the Abrahamic covenant. Another Old Testament scripture that gives details of the New Covenant specifically confirms the fact that a regenerated Israel will live in the Land of Israel:

> I will give you a new heart and put a new spirit
> within you; and I will remove the heart of stone
> from your flesh and give you a heart of flesh. I
> will put My Spirit within you and cause you to

walk in My statutes, and you will be careful to
observe My ordinances. You will live in the land
that I gave to your forefathers; so you will be
My people, and I will be your God
Ezekiel 36:26-28

Paul, in Romans 11, has now explained that part of this consummation involves the national salvation of Israel and the restoration of the nation to the land. Paul used these scriptures from the Old Testament to demonstrate that this is a theme which runs through the Bible and these scriptures have provided a chronological sequence for their fulfilment. They therefore provide a fitting overview of God's redemptive plan for the nation of Israel.

The Regathering and Israel Today

Although a multitude of prophetic scriptures speak of the Jews returning to the Land, there is still great controversy over how these promises are understood. Is the modern State of Israel that exists today the same entity spoken of in these ancient prophecies? What does the future hold for Israel?

The answers to these questions are bound up with the plan of God for Israel. This is why I have endeavoured to provide an outline for a biblical theology of Israel to show the unique

May 16, 1948 edition of Jewish newspaper The Palestine Post, soon renamed into The Jerusalem Post.

place she holds in God's plan. We have already noted the past election of Israel through the Abrahamic covenant and all that goes with this. We know that the covenants still belong to Israel (Romans 9:5) and that the perpetuity of the nation is guaranteed through these covenants – in the words of Jeremiah the prophet, for as long as the sun moon and stars give their light Israel will never cease to be a nation. So how do we understand the regathering of Israel in light of this? The key is to discover that, when speaking of the worldwide regathering of Israel, the Bible distinguishes between *two* worldwide regathering's – one in unbelief, and one in belief. When this is understood it avoids confusion about how to understand the fulfilment of these prophecies

Firstly, the dispersion of the Jewish people across the globe, due to their disobedience, is very clearly taught in the Bible:

> Moreover, the Lord will scatter you among all peoples, from one end of the earth to the other end of the earth; and there you shall serve other gods, wood and stone, which you or your fathers have not known. Among those nations you shall find no rest, and there will be no resting place for the sole of your foot; but there the Lord will give you a trembling heart, failing of eyes, and despair of soul. So your life shall hang in doubt before you; and you will be in dread night and day, and shall have no assurance of your life.
> **Deuteronomy 28:64-66**

This scattering is not into a single nation, like the Babylonian captivity, but "among all the peoples". This event is known as the Diaspora in Jewish history and it happened after the destruction of the Temple in 70 AD. This prophecy in Deuteronomy gives a very good description of how the Jews were, much later, to suffer in their host lands over the years.

So, what of the prophesied return? We see that this shows up in many places throughout the Bible. For instance:

So it shall be when all of these things have come
upon you, the blessing and the curse which
I have set before you, and you call them to
mind in all nations where the Lord your God has
banished you, and you return to the Lord your
God and obey Him with all your heart and
soul according to all that I command you
today, you and your sons, then the Lord your
God will restore you from captivity, and have
compassion on you, and will gather you again
from all the peoples where the Lord your God
has scattered you. If your outcasts are at the
ends of the earth, from there the Lord your God
will gather you, and from there He will bring you
back. The Lord your God will bring you into the
land which your fathers possessed, and you shall
possess it; and He will prosper you and multiply
you more than your fathers.

Deuteronomy 30:1-5

Here the text speaks of a return to the Land after Israel has
first returned to the Lord. This causes confusion, as most
people look at Israel today and see a largely secular nation, one
that is accompanied by all the problems that sin inevitably
brings, and thus they conclude that modern Israel is not the
same as the one depicted in these prophecies. Usually this

results in spiritualising the "Israel" they read about to mean the Church. However, by digging a little deeper into the scriptures the apparent contradiction becomes clear and such an interpretive approach is seen to be inappropriate.

The key text to understand this is Isaiah 11:11-12:

> Then it will happen on that day that the Lord
> Will again recover the second time with His hand
> The remnant of His people, who will remain,
> From Assyria, Egypt, Pathros, Cush, Elam,
> Shinar, Hamath, and from the islands of the sea.
> And He will lift up a standard for the nations
> And assemble the banished ones of Israel,
> And will gather the dispersed of Judah
> From the four corners of the earth.

This regathering of a believing nation in preparation for kingdom blessings is stated here by Isaiah to be the "second" regathering. This second and final regathering takes place along with the second coming of Jesus at the end of the age. This event is often mentioned elsewhere in the Bible, such as Zechariah 12:10:

I will pour out on the house of David and on the
inhabitants of Jerusalem, the Spirit of grace and
of supplication, so that they will look on Me whom
they have pierced; and they will mourn for Him,
as one mourns for an only son, and they will weep
bitterly over Him like the bitter weeping
over a firstborn.

The famous vision of dry bones given by the prophet Ezekiel also speaks of this final blessing for Israel:

"Behold, I will take the sons of Israel from among
the nations where they have gone, and I will
gather them from every side and bring them into
their own land; and I will make them one nation in
the land, on the mountains of Israel; and one king
will be king for all of them; and they will no longer
be two nations and no longer be divided into two
kingdoms. They will no longer defile themselves
with their idols, or with their detestable things, or
with any of their transgressions; but I will deliver
them from all their dwelling places in which they
have sinned, and will cleanse them. And they will
be My people, and I will be their God."
Ezekiel 37:21-23

If this final regathering in Isaiah 11:11 is referred to as the second, then the first must have taken place previously. The only other world-wide regathering of the Jewish people is the regathering in unbelief that has been taking place since 1948. The scriptures also confirm this:

> "As I live," declares the Lord God, "surely with a mighty hand and with an outstretched arm and with wrath poured out, I shall be king over you. I will bring you out from the peoples and gather you from the lands where you are scattered, with a mighty hand and with an outstretched arm and with wrath poured out; and I will bring you into the wilderness of the peoples, and there I will enter into judgment with you face to face."
> **Ezekiel 20: 33-35**

Note that this regathering is done "with wrath poured out" and for the purpose of God "entering into judgement" with His people. This is a regathering that precedes a period of judgement for Israel. The final national redemption of Israel is like a final rebirth of the nation. Yet before the "birth" there is a time of trouble that is to come upon the world. These calamities of the end times are referred to as the birth pangs of the Messiah. Jesus refers to them in His Olivet discourse (Matthew 24:8). The Apostle Paul also refers to them when teaching about the end of days, often referred to as The Day of the Lord:

> While they are saying, "Peace and safety!"
> then destruction will come upon them suddenly
> like labour pains upon a woman with child,
> and they will not escape
> **1 Thessalonians 5:3**

This is a time that will draw the present age to a close, a time, according to Jewish tradition, when the footsteps of the Messiah will be heard. This period will be one of great upheaval and struggle for the Jewish people. The prophet Jeremiah refers to it as "the time of Jacob's trouble" (Jeremiah 30:7) and a time when all the nations of the world will be gathered against Jerusalem (Zechariah 12:3). Yet, although this is uniquely a time of Jacob's trouble, the purpose is ultimately redemptive, for Jeremiah also says, "But he [Jacob] will be saved out of it" (30:7).

Just as in child birth, the baby has a relatively peaceful existence protected in the womb, until the contractions or birth pangs start, and then begins the harsh transition from the womb into the world, so it will be as the world transitions from this age to the Messianic Kingdom age. There will ultimately be a time when the Jewish people will cry out to the Lord to deliver them. Just as Jesus predicted in Matthew 23:39, the people will cry *"Baruch ha ba be shem Adonai!* – Blessed is He who comes in the name of the Lord!" This is when Jesus (Yeshua) will return and destroy those nations that have put themselves in opposition to Israel at this time. Then will come the national salvation of Israel as Ezekiel prophesied:

> Then I will sprinkle clean water on you, and you will be clean; I will cleanse you from all your filthiness and from all your idols. Moreover, I will give you a new heart and put a new spirit within you; and I will remove the heart of stone from your flesh and give you a heart of flesh. I will put My Spirit within you and cause you to walk in My statutes, and you will be careful to observe My ordinances. You will live in the land that I gave to your forefathers; so you will be My people, and I will be your God.
> **Ezekiel 36:25-28**

One thing that we can take away from these prophetic scriptures is that the nation of Israel needed (and still needs) to exist in the Land for many of these prophecies to be fulfilled. Therefore, we must conclude that the present Jewish State, albeit a secular and mostly unbelieving nation, still holds biblical prophetic significance in the plan of God.

Zion – The Eternal City

A multitude of witnesses attest to this fact:

"The view of Jerusalem is the history of the world; it is more, it is the history of earth and of heaven."
Benjamin Disraeli

"You're shaking … so am I. It's because of Jerusalem, isn't it? One doesn't go to Jerusalem, one returns to it. That's one of its mysteries."
Elie Wiesel

"You ought to let the Jews have Jerusalem; it was they who made it famous."
Winston Churchill

"Eternity means Jerusalem."
Talmud, Tractate Berachot 58a

"By far the most distinguished city not in Judea only, but of the whole Orient."
Pliny

"Of the ten measures of beauty that God hath bestowed upon the world, nine of these fall to the lot of Jerusalem."
The Talmud (Kiddushin 49b)

"Erets Yisrael is the navel of the world, and Jerusalem is its centre, and the Bet ha Mikdash is at the centre of Jerusalem, and the Holy of Holies is at its centre, and the Holy Ark is at the centre of the Holy of holies, and in front of it is the Foundation Stone on which the world was founded."
The Midrash Rabbah

These statements, uttered by so many different people, emphasise the important role that the city of Jerusalem has played in Jewish history. Jerusalem has been significant to the religious and cultural life of the Jewish people for thousands of years. Today, the question of Jerusalem is fraught with political complications, conflicting religious worldviews and various disputes over ownership. Yet the controversy of Zion extends far beyond the borders of Israel. The question of Jerusalem has cast a long shadow over the world since its early days as a small city in the hill country of Judah. One just simply needs to walk the ancient streets to get a feel for the history of the city. There are places where the present-day street level is around 90 ft above the ancient city's streets. Layer upon layer of archaeological history lies underfoot – her story is told in the ground – from Jebusite beginnings, to Jewish, Roman, Byzantine, Arab, Crusader, Turkish, and British rule – then finally and miraculously, back into Jewish hands.

Without question there is something unique about this ancient city. In *Jerusalem: The Biography* Simon Montefiore puts it like this:

> "Jerusalem is the house of the one God, the capital of two peoples, the temple of three religions and she is the only city to exist twice— in heaven and on earth: the peerless grace of the terrestrial is as nothing to the glories of the celestial."[20]

The city has countless songs penned in her honour, and still to this day countless numbers of pilgrims and tourists flock through her ancient gates. Armies have marched to conquer her, and soldiers died in defending her. Different nations and different religions all claim heritage and possession of Jerusalem. Even today the United Nations and leaders from around the world involve themselves in the affairs of Jerusalem. Jewish claims to Jerusalem as the capital of the nation state still evoke fierce reactions from groups around the globe. [21]

Although there are many conflicting views and opinions as to why the city of Jerusalem has garnered such international attention, Christians need to ask what the Bible has to say about this ancient city. To factor the city of Zion into a biblical theology of Israel, the scriptures of Israel must be foundational.

The uniqueness of Jerusalem comes neither from its location, nor its historical pedigree, nor its residents. Rather, historically it comes from its position as the capital city of Israel, the people specially chosen by God, where the throne of King David was located. Moreover, it is more than just a site of a huge historical significance (the throne of an ancient kingdom). Jerusalem was chosen as the city where God Himself would come to dwell. For thousands of years the Jewish Temple was the beating heart of this amazing city. The Bible frequently speaks of Jerusalem. Jerusalem is mentioned 800 times in the Bible, with over half of those references being prophetic in nature – strongly indicating a crucially important future for this city.[22] The Bible is very clear that Jerusalem is a chosen city. God declares, "I have chosen Jerusalem that my name may be there..." (2 Chronicles 6:6), and God declares that, "'This is Jerusalem; I have set her at the centre of the nations, with lands around her" (Ezekiel 5:5). Jerusalem continues to occupy this central place throughout the Bible. King David set up his capital in Jerusalem and brought the Ark of the covenant into Jerusalem. This is where his son Solomon reigned during the height of the kingdom, when the nations heard of his fame throughout the world. Although Israel has at times been disciplined by the Lord and removed from the Land into captivity, the heart of the people always longed for Jerusalem:

By the rivers of Babylon,
There we sat down and wept,
When we remembered Zion.
Upon the willows in the midst of it
We hung our harps.
For there our captors demanded of us songs,
And our tormentors mirth, saying,
"Sing us one of the songs of Zion."
How can we sing the Lord's song
In a foreign land?
If I forget you, O Jerusalem,
May my right hand forget her skill.
May my tongue cling to the roof of my mouth
If I do not remember you,
If I do not exalt Jerusalem
Above my chief joy.
Psalm 137:1-6

The Old Testament places Jerusalem as the very center of its redemptive story. It is where the sacrificial system operated, and atonement was made for the people's sins. The Mosaic Law required Jewish pilgrims to journey up to Jerusalem to celebrate the feasts of Passover (Pesach), Pentecost (Shavuot) and Tabernacles (Sukkot). One of these young pilgrims was the boy Yeshua, faithfully brought to the feasts by his parents Mary and Joseph every year (Luke 2:41-51).

The New Testament also places Jerusalem at the very heart of the gospel story. It is here that Jesus gave some of His most famous teaching: the sermon on the Mount of Olives, the proclamation at the feast of Tabernacles that whoever believes in Him, from his innermost being "will flow rivers of living water" (John 7:38). Here He instituted the ordinance of communion at the last supper Passover meal. During those final days as He walked upwards towards Jerusalem, and he caught a glimpse of the city it says, "He saw the city and wept over it," (Luke 19:41). He wept at the Garden of Gethsemane as he prepared to go to the cross. On the third day after His suffering it was from a tomb in Jerusalem that He was raised to new life. Jerusalem was the setting for the events that form the foundation of the gospel. Finally, after these momentous events, the Church was born in Jerusalem by the power of the Holy Spirit, and from Jerusalem the message of the gospel spread throughout the world.

Although Jerusalem has a long and colourful past we know that there still awaits a glorious future for this city and its people. One day it will take its place as the head of all nations and the capital of all capitals when Messiah sits on His throne in her ancient gates and rules His Kingdom.

In the latter days the prophets predict that the issue of Jerusalem will be an international problem:

Behold, I am going to make Jerusalem a cup that
causes reeling to all the peoples around; and
when the siege is against Jerusalem, it will also
be against Judah. It will come about in that day
that I will make Jerusalem a heavy stone for all
the peoples; all who lift it will be severely injured.
And all the nations of the earth will
be gathered against it.
Zechariah 12:2-3

As the international tide turns against the city of Jerusalem and
her enemies plot her demise, the Lord says "For I will gather all
the nations against Jerusalem to battle" (Zechariah 14:2), and
on that day He will go forth and fight against those nations
(14:3); this is when, in the midst of Christ's triumphant
return to rescue His people, He will descend on the clouds of
heaven to the Mount of Olives:

In that day His feet will stand on the Mount of
Olives, which is in front of Jerusalem on the east
Zechariah 14:4

Then, finally the reign of the Messianic King will commence,
and no one shall challenge his rule:

> And the Lord will be king over all the earth;
> in that day the Lord will be the only one,
> and His name the only one
> **Zechariah 14:9**

From this ancient city the Messianic King will rule with justice over the nations. The prophet Isaiah records a vision of this wonderful day when the nations will stream up to Jerusalem to inquire of the ways of the Lord. From there, Jesus will render decisions and instruct the people from His Word. It will be a time of universal peace and prosperity when the nations will no longer learn war.

> Now it will come about that in the last days
> the mountain of the house of the Lord will be
> established as the chief of the mountains,
> and will be raised above the hills; and all the
> nations will stream to it. And many peoples
> will come and say, "Come, let us go up to the
> mountain of the Lord, to the house of the God of
> Jacob; that He may teach us concerning His ways
> and that we may walk in His paths."
> For the law will go forth from Zion and the word
> of the Lord from Jerusalem. And He will judge
> between the nations, and will render decisions for
> many peoples; and they will hammer their swords

into plowshares and their spears into pruning
hooks. Nation will not lift up sword against nation,
and never again will they learn war.
Isaiah 2:1-4

At this time Habakkuk proclaims that the earth shall be filled with the knowledge of the glory of the Lord as the waters cover the sea (Habakkuk 2:14). There has never been, nor will there ever be, a city like Jerusalem.

Truth Four:

Unbelieving *Israel* is still beloved for the sake of the fathers

> From the standpoint of the gospel they are
> enemies for your sake, but from the standpoint
> of God's choice, they are beloved for the
> sake of the fathers
> **Romans 11:28**

What initially might seem like a contradictory statement is in fact a fitting conclusion for the thoughts that precede it. This verse contains a vital truth for Christians to understand today. It will impact how Christians interact with unbelieving Jews. Paul here gives a clear summary of Israel's dual status and how it relates to the main thrust of the argument that he is addressing in chapters 9–11. National corporate Israel, which even now is hardened toward the gospel and in a state of enmity toward God, being described as an "enemy", is not completely rejected. Rather, whilst being described in this way they are equally designated as "beloved" – they are Christians' "beloved enemy". The Church is to understand that this present state of hardening was necessary in order for salvation to come to the Gentiles. Paul previously affirmed that "they did not stumble so as to fall, did they? May it never be! But by their transgression salvation has come to the Gentiles, to make them jealous!" (11:11). The natural branches have been broken off and the Gentiles, as "wild olive" branches, have now been grafted into "the rich root of the olive tree" (11:17).

Given this situation, the Gentiles must be careful not to become arrogant toward the "natural branches" (11:21,24). In fact, the Apostle Paul argues that, "because of the mercy shown to you [Gentiles] they [Jews] also may now be shown mercy" (11:31). The mercy talked about here is gospel mercy. Gentile Christians who have received the gospel at the expense of branches of national Israel being broken off, should now be active in Jewish evangelism. However, the apostle elsewhere argues that the gentile Church's attitude towards unbelieving Israel should exceed evangelism only and display itself in an attitude of love that is concerned with physical blessings too. He argues, "For if the Gentiles have shared in their spiritual things, they are indebted to minister to them also in material things" (Romans 15:27). Therefore, the attitude of the Church towards unbelieving Jews should be focused around the gospel yet at the same time this love should be manifested by acts of practical love which accurately display the heart of Jesus towards his people.

With this in mind, it is important to understand how a Church that has become arrogant against the natural branches because of their unbelief, or a Church whose theology on Israel is ill-conceived—or worse, antisemitic—stands little chance of provoking Israel into a state of jealousy. Can the doctrine of

TRUTH FOUR

replacement theology with its teaching of eternal rejection and replacement for the Jewish people really provoke them to jealousy? Surely such a belief will lead to a neglect of interest in the plight of the Jewish people around the world at best, and outright negativity at worst? Tragically, the history of the Church testifies that this is often the case.

How Can we Bless Israel?

The Gospel

In light of the theology discussed in the preceding section it is important that the Church thinks clearly about what it means to properly bless the people of Israel. Unfortunately, many have seen this command as simply a call to support Jewish charities or secular initiatives in Israel. These may be commendable causes and worthy of support, but they cannot be seen as the primary fulfilment of what it means for the Church to bless Israel. We must avoid any simplistic understanding which causes blind allegiance to anything overtly Jewish, as is often the case in evangelical churches that support Israel. We need to be clear that the greatest need for the people of Israel is that they recognise Jesus as their Messiah. This was the heart of the Apostle Paul who said, "my heart's desire and my prayer to God for them is for their salvation" (Romans 10:1). This should be our attitude too.

This will entail their acknowledgement that Rabbinic or Talmudic Judaism is not sufficient to save them – they need the gospel of Yeshua preached to them. This means that the Church should be supporting those ministries that are actively involved in taking the good news of Messiah to the Jewish people, not merely those who provide humanitarian support, much of which, unfortunately, is actively funnelled away from Messianic Jews in the land of Israel.

There is a biblical mandate for financial support to the Jewish believers given in Romans 15, which talks about the contribution from Macedonia and Achaia for the poor saints in Jerusalem. This is a good model for churches today. To be active in supporting the body of Christ in Israel in addition to supporting Jewish evangelism worldwide.[23]

An Example from History

The famous missionary Hudson Taylor, born in a small town in Yorkshire in 1832, became the founder of the *China Inland Mission* (now *Overseas Missionary Fellowship*). He established hundreds of churches and schools and became a spiritual father to millions of Chinese Christians. Although he clearly followed a call to reach the Chinese people with the gospel and was successful in doing that, he still understood the priority of Jewish evangelism. Much like the Apostle Paul, who was

From A Retrospect by James Hudson Taylor 1893 Morgan & Scott.

called to reach the Gentiles, Taylor always operated under the principle in Romans 1:16 that the gospel is "to the Jew first". He would begin each year by writing a cheque to John Wilkinson, the founder of one of the largest Jewish mission societies at that time, the *Mildmay Mission to the Jews* in London. Accompanying the cheque would inevitably be a note on which he had written, "to the Jew first". Mr Wilkinson would immediately reply by enclosing his own cheque for the same amount with a note, "and also to the gentile". This beautiful exchange continued indefinitely between these two men and it is a great testimony to us today.

I believe that the actions of Hudson Taylor and John Wilkinson are in no small part responsible for the fruitfulness of the missionary organisations they started. Their attitudes clearly reflect the biblical heart for missionary work among God's people and the proper application of God's original promise in Genesis that says, "I will bless those who bless you..." (Genesis 12:3).

Prayer

As we have seen, the Apostle Paul prayed for the salvation of Israel, and this should be a continual prayer of the Church today. The psalmist also declares, "pray for the peace of Jerusalem: 'May they prosper that love you'" (Psalm 122:6). Ultimately, we know peace will only come to Jerusalem when the Messiah returns. Until then we pray for the peace that the gospel brings into the Land of Israel by transforming hearts and minds. However, there are additional practical ways we can pray for Israel. We can pray for safety and security of those in the Land, we can pray for the leaders and government of Israel, particularly with regard to those who actively hinder the spread of the gospel in Israel. The Church should intercede that media coverage about Israel would be true; far too often, nefarious lies are told that cast Israel in a bad light. We should also pray for the governments of our own countries to be fair in their dealing with Israel. These are just a few ways we can bless Israel through intercessory prayer.

Provoke them to Jealousy

The Gentile Church is meant to provoke the Jews to jealousy, just as Paul did (Romans 11:11). This means that the very fact that we are in relationship with the God of Israel through the Jewish Messiah should cause the Jewish people to want that same relationship. Tragically, segments of the Church have at times displayed to the Jewish people a faith that actively persecutes and denounces them, hardly likely to produce a desire to follow this faith. The legacy of antisemitism within Christendom is something that needs to be confronted and strongly opposed. The Church needs to root out any last vestiges of theological antisemitism that still remain in its ranks, as well as refuting false libels and accusations against the Jewish people. In fact, the Church needs to do more than just stand against antisemitism, it needs to display a positive attitude of genuine philo-semitism[24] – one that flows naturally and consistently from the roots of our faith and accurately represents the heart of Jesus.

Truth Five:

The *Promises* given to Israel are irrevocable

5

For the gifts and the calling of
God are irrevocable
Romans 11:29

Paul has argued that Israel remains important in God's plan based upon the promises given to the patriarchs. As we have seen in this booklet these promises cover such a huge portion of the biblical narrative that to ignore them or spiritualise them away will not do justice to Scripture. The promises of God to Israel clearly speak of things that have yet to be fulfilled and here, the apostle makes the argument that we can have confidence in their fulfilment because when God makes a promise, He keeps it!

As long as those promises stand, then so does Paul's argument concerning the future of national Israel. He confirms this simply by announcing that the gifts and calling of God are irrevocable (binding, irreversible). It is best to see the phrase "calling" here as referring to the election of Israel as a nation, which ultimately was to be a light to the nations:

And now says the Lord, who formed Me from the
womb to be His Servant, to bring Jacob back to
Him, so that Israel might be gathered to Him (For I
am honored in the sight of the Lord, and My God is
My strength), He says, "It is too small a thing that
You should be My Servant to raise up the tribes of
Jacob and to restore the preserved ones of Israel; I
will also make You a light of the nations So that My
salvation may reach to the end of the earth."
Isaiah 49:5-6

The term "gifts" is best identified as encompassing all the
privileges and blessings that go with this election. They include
many of the things Paul lists in Romans 9:5, the covenants
and the promises associated with them. This would include
the land promises given to Israel. The term "irrevocable" also
carries with it the idea that something cannot be undone or
changed. The term is translated as "without repentance" in the
King James version, giving the idea that God does not change
His mind. Paul is making the point that God has not changed
His mind about the gifts and calling of Israel, they are still very
much within His plan for the future. The promises of God
concerning Israel are certain, they will undergo a national
regeneration and regathering, for the Word of God cannot be
broken; His promises are sure.

The Jewish King

One day, the one who was ethnically born a Jew will rule the world as King of Kings and Lord of Lords! – this is the ultimate conclusion of the gospel story. He will be the greatest monarch that has ever set foot upon this earth. A descendant of the line of David, of the tribe of Judah. A King whose reign will be characterised by love, mercy, compassion and holiness. Indeed, the very foundation of His throne will be "righteousness and justice" (Psalm 89:44). There shall be no one worthy to challenge His rule, no one with greater wisdom, nor greater love for His subjects. His glory shall cover the earth, and no one will be ignorant of who He is.

Yet the interesting thing to know about this future King is that His glorious future reign will not be the first time He has set foot on this earth. This King is none other than the Messiah foretold in the Jewish scriptures. He will rule for all eternity because He Himself is eternal. The prophet Micah predicts that this future King will be born in Bethlehem and "His goings forth are from long ago, from the days of eternity" (Micah 5:2). This King is not like all other earthly kings because He is also a heavenly King. The prophet Jeremiah talks of this Davidic King:

> "Behold, the days are coming," declares the Lord,
> "When I will raise up for David a righteous Branch;
> and He will reign as king and act wisely and do
> justice and righteousness in the land. In His days
> Judah will be saved, and Israel will dwell securely;
> and this is His name by which He will be called,
> The Lord our righteousness."
> **Jeremiah 23:5-6**

Notice that it is clearly stated at the end of this passage that the Davidic King, who was born in Bethlehem, will also be called the LORD – the holy name of God.

Furthermore, it was announced before time in the scriptures that this Messiah King would enter Jerusalem riding upon a lowly donkey (Zechariah 9:9) as the crowds shouted "Hosanna!" (Mark 11:9, John 12:13). Yet he would be betrayed soon after for thirty pieces of silver (Zechariah 11:12-13).

The Suffering King – Isaiah 53

After His betrayal, the scriptures foretold that the Messiah would be rejected and forsaken by His people and would ultimately die a vicarious death for the sins of the world. He would be "pierced through for our transgressions" (Isaiah 53:5), scourged, chastised and led like a lamb to the slaughter

(53:7). The Lord would cause "the iniquity of us all to fall upon Him" (53:6). The Lord would be pleased to place the punishment for our sins upon His Messiah and "render Him as a guilt offering" (53:10). As a result, this suffering servant "will justify many (53:11)" as "He poured out Himself to death" (53:12) and identified with sinners in order to bear their sins. However, for a King that has power of life, death was not the end, as the psalmist predicts the Lord will not allow His "Holy one to undergo decay" (Psalm 16:10). The King will be raised to new life and ascend back into Glory, waiting for the day when He must return.

One or Two Comings?

The question that many Jewish people have wrestled with over the years is how to harmonise these two very different groups of prophecy about the Messiah. On the one hand He is described as a humiliated and lowly person who will suffer and die, on the other hand He is pictured as a glorious conquering King who will vanquish His enemies. Many theories have been proposed. Some say there are in fact two Messiahs – one in the character of King David and the other in the character of Joseph who was betrayed by his brothers. Many Jews cannot accept that Jesus is the Messiah because, looking around at the world today it does not seem like he accomplished the promise of ushering in an age of peace. Unfortunately, such an analysis does not consider the full scope of biblical revelation that we are given about the mission of the Messiah.

The solution is to understand that there are not two Messiahs, there is only one Messiah, who comes twice. The prophets *do* speak of a conquering King Messiah who will one day come and restore the tabernacle of David, usher in an age of peace and rule from Jerusalem (Amos 9:11). But that will be His *second* coming into this world (his return). Prior to this, the spiritual brokenness which resulted from mankind's rebellion had to be dealt with – men needed a way to make peace with God. It is this that was accomplished by the suffering servant at His *first* coming. He came to die for the sins of the world so that man may be reconciled and have peace with God.

When Did He Come?

The amazing thing is that the scriptures do provide certain time parameters for when the Messiah had to come. This is not to be confused with sensational date-setting for the end of the world or anything like that. The first appearance of the Messiah was predicted to happen within very specific time constraints. A fascinating prophecy in Daniel chapter 9 provides these details, famously known as the "Seventy Weeks" prophecy:

Seventy weeks have been decreed for your people
and your holy city, to finish the transgression,
to make an end of sin, to make atonement for
iniquity, to bring in everlasting righteousness,
to seal up vision and prophecy and to anoint
the most holy place. So you are to know and
discern that from the issuing of a decree to
restore and rebuild Jerusalem until Messiah
the Prince there will be seven weeks and sixty-
two weeks; it will be built again, with plaza and
moat, even in times of distress. Then after the
sixty-two weeks the Messiah will be cut off and
have nothing, and the people of the prince who is
to come will destroy the city and the sanctuary.
Daniel 9:24-26

The Second Jewish Temple. Model in the Israel Museum.
By Anna Beveridge.

Here are the relevant facts we take from this amazing text:

1 **The Messiah will come 483 years (69 x seven 'weeks of years') after the command to rebuild and restore Jerusalem (v. 25).**

2 **The Temple would still be standing when the Messiah arrives.**

3 **Then the Messiah would be cut off (i.e. die a violent death; v. 26).**

4 **After the death of Messiah, Jerusalem and the Temple would be destroyed (v. 26).**

These four facts from the prophet Daniel form an insurmountable argument that the Messiah had to come, *and* be killed, before the destruction of the Temple. The text uses the Jewish reckoning of "weeks" of years (units of seven years) and states that from a specific decree the clock starts ticking. The prophet Daniel lived during the Babylonian exile and the decree mentioned is that of Artaxerxes Longimanus (Nehemiah 2:1-8). Scholars agree that this took place in the month of Nisan in the year 444 BC. If we take this as the starting point and add the 483 years, we come to the year AD 33. So, the prophecy says that the Messiah would appear by the year AD 33.[25]

The text then states that sometime after the Messiah would be "cut off", a phrase meaning killed by a violent death. This matches the description given in Isaiah 53 that the Messiah would die for the sins of the people – "He was cut off out of the land of the living for the transgression of my people" (Isaiah 53:8). Then finally, the Daniel prophecy details that after the execution of the Messiah the city of Jerusalem and the Holy Temple would be destroyed. This event happened in AD 70 when the city was sacked by the Roman forces under Titus Vespasian. We know from this that the Temple must still have been standing when the Messiah was alive. This means that the Messiah had to arrive by the year AD 33 and that he would be killed for the sins of the people before AD 70. That leaves only a very small window of 37 years for all this to be fulfilled.

Historically, there is only one candidate for the Messiah: just one Jewish person who lived at this time, was a descendant of David from the Tribe of Judah, was born in the town of Bethlehem, performed the acts that the Messiah was prophesied to do, identified himself as the Messiah – *and* suffered a violent death before the destruction of the Temple in AD 70. The identification of Yeshua of Nazareth as the Messiah is inescapable.

The Way Forward

Undoubtedly the controversy surrounding Israel will continue, both in the world at large and the Church. Politically the nation of Israel remains in a precarious position, surrounded on all sides by those who desire to see her eradicated. Religiously, within Jerusalem's walls there is an eclectic mix of ancient traditions. Jerusalem is the epicentre of the three monotheistic faiths, and home to a largely secular population who simply desire to live in peace with their neighbours. Security concerns, attempted political solutions and the inevitable clashes from time to time will continue to influence people's opinions on the matter.

The task for the Church is to make sure that we see with spiritual eyes first. This means that we understand the role Israel is to play in God's larger redemptive plan for the nations. Only then can we truly hope to interpret the world around us through the lens of scripture. This booklet has been written to introduce readers to the theology of Israel and thereby to contribute to this effort. It is vitally important that the Church is actively involved in speaking and teaching about these issues in order to help a generation that has become detached from its biblical roots to understand the importance of Israel in the plan of God. It is also important to realise that, having a positive theology of Israel in no way precludes Christians from showing compassion and gospel ministry to the Palestinians, and all inhabitants of the Middle East for that matter.

Yet this work has been specifically concerned with outlining a positive biblical theology of Israel in order to help people understand the times and to correct the error of replacement theology that has plagued the Church for so long. I hope it will help ensure that the negative consequences that have flowed from this over the centuries will not be repeated by the Church.

It is imperative that the Church models the heart of the Apostle Paul for Israel, who wished that he himself could be cut off it meant that his people would be saved (Romans 9:3). In the same way that Jesus wept over His people's unbelief in Jerusalem, we should weep over unbelieving Israel at this time. The Church should have a theology that acknowledges the future role of Israel in the plan of God and actively promotes Jewish evangelism, while simultaneously standing against both theological and political antisemitism. A rich, robust theology such as this will contribute to the global health of the Church which, in the larger picture, will also mean that the message of the Jewish King goes out to all the nations.

Maranatha!

Wake Harp of Zion

Wake, harp of Zion, wake again,
Upon thine ancient hill,
On Jordan's long deserted plain,
By Kedron's lowly rill.
The hymn shall yet in Zion swell,
That sounds Messiah's praise,
And thy loved name, Emmanuel,
As once in ancient days.
For Israel yet shall own her king,
For her salvation waits,
And hill and dale shall sweetly sing,
With praise in all her gates.
O hasten, Lord, these promised days,
When Israel shall rejoice,
And Jew and Gentile join in praise,
With one united voice!

James Edmeston (1846)

Endnotes

1   Baruch Maoz. "People, Land and Torah: a Jewish Christian Perspective", in: Johnston, P and Walker, P; *The Land of Promise: Biblical, Theological and Contemporary Perspectives*. (Downer Grove: Intervarsity 2000) pg. 191.

2   Ernst Frankenstein. *Justice for My People: The Jewish Case* (London: Nicholson & Watson, 1943) pg. 79.

3   Leo Tolstoy, *What is the Jew?* printed in Jewish World periodical, 1908.

4   The Talmudic era of Judaism is usually considered to be between 200 – 500 CE

5   Mark Twain, *Concerning the Jews*, Harper's Magazine, 1899.

6   Darrell L. Bock and Mitch Glaser (Eds). *Israel, the Church, and the Middle East* (Grand Rapids, MI: Kregel Publications, 2018) pg. 230.

7   Michael J. Vlach. Has the Church Replaced Israel? (Nashville: B&H Publishing, 2010) pg. 5.

8   Dennis Prager and Joseph Telushkin. *Why the Jews: The Reason for Anti-Semitism* (New York: Touchstone, 2003) pg. 87.

9   Ibid pg. 92.

10   Christendom being a more generic term applying to countries where Christianity is the dominant religion. Often used to refer to the period of the Church under Roman Catholic rule during the Middle ages. However, being part of Christendom does not necessarily mean a true biblical faith is included.

11   Fred Wright. *Words from the Scroll of Fire*. (Jerusalem: Four Corners Publishing, 1994) pg. 104-105.

12   Dan Cohn-Sherbok. *Anti-Semitism* (Gloucestershire: The History Press, 2009) pg. 90.

13   Phillips, M. Christians Who Hate Jews, *The Spectator* (16 February 2002).

14   Sam Sokol. Robert Wistrich, Leading scholar of Anti-Semitism dies of heart attack, Jerusalem Post.

15   The Birkat HaMinin has roots in early Second Temple Judaism and was largely used to root out Sadduceeism and Boethians, not just Christian Jews.

16   D. Instone-Brewer. The Eighteen Benedictions and the Minim Before 70 CE, *Journal of Theological Studies* 54, no. 1 (2003): 25–24.

17   Christine Graef. *The Jewish Concern for the Church: How far have we drifted from the one new humanity the Apostles envisioned* (Oregon: Wipf & Stock, 2017) pg. 16.

18   Douglas Moo. The Epistle to the Romans, *NICNT* (Grand Rapids: William B. Eerdmans Publishing Co., 1996) pg. 717.

19   J.C.Ryle. *Are you Ready for the End Time?* (Fearn, Scotland: Christian Focus, 2001), pg. 183.

20   Simon Sebag Montefiore. *Jerusalem: The Biography* (London: Weidenfeld & Nicolson, 2011) preface.

21   For example, the reaction when President Trump announced that the United States recognised Jerusalem as the capital of Israel on 6th December 2017.

22   Randall Price. *Jerusalem in Prophecy: God's stage for the final Drama* (Eugene, OR: Harvest House Publishers, 1998) pg. 78-79.

23   This principle is also properly applied to all churches to be on the lookout to support all believers in material need (cf. Galatians 6:10).

24   Philo is the Greek word for love.

25   Based upon the 360-day prophetic year calendar used by Israel in the time of Daniel the prophet.

About the Author

Thomas Fretwell is the founder and director of the Ezra Foundation. He holds both B.Th. and M.A. Degrees in Theology and is currently undertaking Ph.D. research in a field related to Jewish-Christian Studies. He is a tutor in Theology at King's Evangelical Divinity School where he teaches courses on Israel, Politics, and the Land for the schools Jewish-Christian Study Centre. Thomas regularly speaks to people of all ages on a variety of biblical topics and apologetics issues. He hosts the Theology & Apologetics podcast and is the Pastor of Calvary Chapel Hastings in the UK.

The Ezra Foundation exists to encourage and facilitate the serious study of the Word of God by producing resources that promote a biblical understanding of Israel in the plan of God.

For more information please go to:

EZRAFOUNDATION.ORG

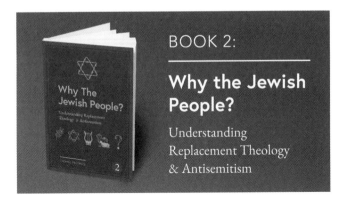

BOOK 2:

Why the Jewish People?

Understanding
Replacement Theology
& Antisemitism

The Bible teaching ministry of

THOMAS FRETWELL
B.Th., M.A, Ph.D student

For audio talks, publications, blog, podcast and speaking schedule visit
theologyandapologetics.com

theology.apologetics

Human Identity and the Gospel in a Confusing World - What does it mean to be human? - What is it that makes us so unique? - Is there any meaning to life?

This book will provide those answers by examining human nature in light of the Word of God. It will demonstrate the difference the Gospel message makes in the way you understand human identity.